Get Sideways

The short guide to navigating the Santa Ynez Valley Wine Country

Get Sideways

The short guide to navigating the Santa Ynez Valley Wine Country

Shelly Cone

Table of Contents

Introduction

Of all the places I've lived in California, the Santa Ynez Valley remains one of my favorites. It's oak-studded hills and rows upon rows of wine grapes appear in the backdrop whenever I try to conjure up the most "perfect place in the world."

My husband proposed to me in the Valley in a usually quiet restaurant made even more memorable by the unexpected convergence of raucous bicyclists just having completed the Solvang Century. We married under a majestic oak tree in the lawn of a beautiful winery set in a centuries-old adobe building.

I was drinking coffee and taking in the breathtaking view out of my kitchen window the day the Valley got its first, and extremely rare, snowfall in decades.

I've spent many a blistery afternoon playing the River Course at the Alisal when we lived just across the street and spent many hours perusing the downtown Solvang shops when I had nothing in particular to do but enjoy my neighborhood.

And lets not forget the countless wine tasting occasions.

No doubt my bond to the Valley has made me somewhat biased, however, I've watched the area blossom like its very own wine grapes, into a well-respected wine region. I challenge anyone to experience the Valley and its offerings and argue against its beauty and serenity.

The popularity of the recent movie *Sideways*, which showcased the Valley, has shone a spotlight on my secret getaway. This guide is for those readers who were introduced to the Valley via the movie. It is by no means all-inclusive of "what's good" in the Valley, but more of a guide for those who want to take the "*Sideways* tour" of the Valley.

Overview

There is nothing that is not exquisite about the Santa Ynez Valley – a secret gem nestled at the base of the Santa Ynez Mountains that has only recently received notoriety, primarily because of the release of the movies *Sideways*. The movie was almost entirely shot in the Santa Ynez Valley, portraying two men on a quest for meaning as they head sideways into a mid-life crisis.

Santa Ynez Valley is only a 2 ½-hour drive north of the crowds and traffic of Los Angeles but feels like it's a world away. It's a hidden haven of quiet and nature but boasts enough attractions to make it a destination for travelers.

The most striking thing about the Valley is its landscape. Rolling hills are green in the spring, evoking images of Ireland, and then turn gold in the summer. Oak trees dot the terrain occasionally interrupting vast rows of wine grapevines.

Winding, scenic roads twist their way past an abundance of rustic wineries. The Valley considers itself wine country, offering award-winning and nationally renowned wines and making the area a smaller version of the Napa Valley.

The Valley has long been a hideaway for the rich and fabulous but why it hasn't gained more attention before the release of *Sideways* is beyond me.

Warm weather, delicious scenery and world-class wines are only a few of the region's offerings.

If you want to take a *Sideways* adventure, get ready to roll down your window, let the wind whip your hair and lean back.

Orientation

Anchoring the Santa Ynez Valley, is the small town of Solvang. Dubbed the Danish Capital of America, Solvang hasn't lost its sense of origin. The city was founded by Danish immigrants, who called the place Solvang – meaning sunny field. The place quickly grew and attracted more Danish immigrants.

The city's architecture keeps with its Northern European heritage. All businesses and buildings maintain the "Danish" look. Tiny, sparkling white lights strung along buildings and trees throughout the downtown, stay lit year-round giving it a magical feel. Stroll the many unique shops and eateries during the day and take an evening walk under the starts to work off those Danish pastries.

Solvang also hosts a number of winery tasting rooms in its downtown area – just a few stumbles away from many hotels.

Solvang is surrounded by the towns of Santa Ynez, Los Olivos, Buellton and Ballard. If you take one of the two-lane winding roads out of Solvang, it'll take you past Ballard and several apple orchards, where you can stop and pick the fruit yourself. Many wineries are tucked away on the outskirts of Solvang as well.

A couple of miles of softly winding road will take you to Los Olivos, where you can shop for antiques or walk around several tasting rooms. Nearby the western-themed Santa Ynez boasts more antiques and some excellent gourmet restaurants that'll get your taste buds going. For breakfast you can't miss a stop in Buellton and **Ellen's Danish Pancake House, 272 Avenue of the Flags, (805) 688-5312.**

Getting There, the Sights of Sideways Country

From the north or the south, Highway 101 will lead you straight to Buellton. Coming from Lompoc in the west take Highway 246 straight into town (once in Solvang, Highway 246 turns into Mission Drive.) From Buellton, Highway 246 will lead you into the heart of Solvang.

If you've already seen the movie *Sideways* you'll instantly recognize the Days Inn "Windmill Inn" hotel at the Solvang off ramp from Highway 101. About ½ mile up the road headed toward Solvang, you'll pass the infamous Hitching Post restaurant on your right, where Jack and Miles spent much of their time. A.J. Spurs is right next-door.

You'll pass the Ostrich Farm and a short stretch of ranches before coming to a halt behind a line of cars coming into Solvang.

Not to worry though, you're entering Solvang's main drag, which has a much slower speed limit. Generally it's the rubbernecking by tourists that slows things down even more. Even so, it's not the big city and traffic will continue moving, just a bit slower. Just relax and remember a very fruitful exploration awaits.

Weather

The Valley is typically hot during the day but can cool off considerably (into the 60s) in the evening during the summer months. Average summer day temps hover around the mid 80s and can easily get into the 90s, so dress lightly, but bring a sweater. The Santa Ynez Mountains that surround the Valley are one of the few ranges that face east/west. This causes a funnel effect drawing cool air from the ocean at night. This same effect is what makes the region great for the Pinot Noir, Syrah and Chardonnay that thrive here.

Winter months are cooler and a thick jacket will be appreciated if you are doing a lot of outside touring.

Getting Around

It's ideal to take a full day or two to explore Solvang itself and maybe a full day to cruise through the rest of the Valley. Solvang is definitely a place you need to walk. Streets are narrow and there are many tourists criss-crossing streets. Everything is in the compact downtown area, making a car unnecessary.

If you do drive around downtown, note that it's tough to make a left turn on some of the downtown intersections, even at the lights. The best lights to make a left turn are toward either edge of town.

A park in the middle of downtown offers weary walkers plenty of shade, lots of seating and a place to people watch. After you catch your breath you may decide to tour the city by bike. Surrey bike rentals are popular. If you're not familiar with them they are covered bikes that have enough seating for a small family, most even have a small bench up front for little children.

If you stay in Solvang you will need a car to explore the surrounding communities, or if you are physically fit, the area is popular with bicyclists for its challenging roads and its scenic beauty.

Where to Stay

You can't go wrong staying anywhere is Solvang, simply because you're right in the middle of everything. Downtown Solvang has a number of tasting rooms along Copenhagen and Mission drives within walking distance of each other, shops and hotels, so a Solvang hotel is convenient when you've had a little too much tasting downtown.

If you're here for a romantic getaway, try the **Storybook Inn Bed and Breakfast, 409 First Street, (805) 688-1703** (http://www.solvangstorybook.com/) It's a bed and breakfast located ½ block off of Copenhagen Drive, nestled in a quiet neighborhood, but a minute or two walking to shops.

Wine Valley Inn & Cottages, 1564 Copenhagen Drive, Solvang, 688-2111 (http://www.winevalleyinn.com/) is another romantic locale in town offering 51 guest rooms and six individual cottages surrounded by meandering gardens. The Inn is surrounded by shopping and restaurants.

If family is in tow my favorite is the **Vagabond Inn, 1450 Mission Drive, Solvang, (805) 688-3210**. The unassuming place looks as simple from the outside as it is inside – but it boasts a surprise. It features a recreation room with a large indoor heated pool, video games, a fireplace and plenty of tables to sit and enjoy a late night pizza.

At the entrance to Solvang, it's still just about a five minute walk downtown but right next door to the Solvang Market, which is convenient for that late night beer or liquor run or diaper dash.

In the movie Jack and Miles stay at the **Days Inn "Windmill Inn," 114 E. Highway 246, in Buellton, (805) 688-8448**, another favorite of mine.

Of course it's easily identifiable by its obvious wooden windmill that can be seen from the freeway. Again, the rooms are simple, rates reasonable and most rooms overlook the pool. The hotel features a sports bar on the premise, frequented by a lot of locals. Watch the game, hang around the bar or play a game of pool – that is if you can find the time.

Where to Eat

Jack and Miles ate mostly at the Hitching Post but also visited A.J. Spurs and Los Olivos Café. All fabulous places. *If you plan on retracing their footsteps a word of advice – make reservations, you won't be the only ones wanting to have your picture taken outside the Hitching Post sign.* And with the movie's popularity those restaurants already have seen an increase in patrons. But they are well worth the preparation.

However, there are many more excellent restaurants. Try the classy **Café Angelica, 490 First Streets, Ste. A, Solvang, (805) 686-9970** for an Italian-flavored lunch. The ambience is a little more refined; it's a cozy place in the heart of Solvang with limited outdoor seating. Probably not the best kids place – if your kids are like mine.

That award would have to go to A.J. Spurs, **350 E. Highway 246, Buellton, (805) 686-1655,** (http://www.ajspurs.com/) hands down. A.J.'s has a jubilant (read noisy, but in a good way) atmosphere filled with people talking and laughing, plates clanging and the crackle of a fireplace. Decorated in antique Western items like spurs and branding irons, the décor provides plenty to talk about.

Hefty portions of food, a complimentary after-dinner liqueur, or milk shake for the kids, and a giant stuffed buffalo greeting you at the door round out an evening at A.J.s. The little cowpokes enjoy dipping into the treasure chest on their way out.

For real cowboys – and girls, A.J.s features a small bar with weekend entertainment and serving the regular bar fare (think buffalo wings.)

Next door at the **Hitching Post, 406 E. Highway 246, Buellton, (805) 688-0676** (http://www.hitchingpost2.com/) you won't find Maya there, but you will get a great meal and wonderful wine. Please, order a steak or ribs, they do them right.

Casual in the daytime, **Los Olivos Café, 2879 Grand Ave., (805) 688-7265**, (http://www.losolivoscafe.com/) is the place to eat in Los Olivos. They even have a Sideways special if you want to eat like the characters did. With an extensive selection of wine and serving California-Mediterranean cuisine, the café is a local favorite. It's also a rather cozy place with some outdoor seating.

The Red Barn Steak House, 3539 Sagunto St., (805) 688-4142, in Santa Ynez is another unassuming place that serves a wonderful salmon or steak.

Here's a local secret. If you're simply looking for a quick bite, head to Shelbi Ranch in downtown Solvang on First Street, a block off of Copenhagen. Everything on the menu is a buck. Hot dogs, hamburgers, lemonade – and the food is actually pretty tasty. Decked out in old Hollywood Western memorabilia you can also find T-shirts, jeans and sundresses for a steal (try the $1-$5 range).

Golf

In the movie the guys golfed the **River Course at the Alisal, 150 Alisal Road, Solvang, (805) 688-6042**. The course offers expansive mountain views, and a wonderful restaurant with patio seating overlooking the course. The Alisal also offers a private course called the Ranch Course, mainly for guests of the ranch.

For a more laid back afternoon on the course, try **Zaca Creek Golf Course, 223 Shadow Mountain Drive in Buellton, (805) 688-2575**. The greens may not always be as green as the Alisal but the easy nine-hole course is perfect for trying out the game. You'll often even see young children on the course getting coached by their dads.

This course offers straight fairways, scenic mountain views and golfers that are there for the love of the sport, not necessarily worried about shaving an extra stroke from their game.

And most of the time, when there's no tournament, you don't even need to schedule a tee time. It's a walking course, however, there are carts available and it's a rather small course making the walking pretty easy.

The Wineries

There are several approaches to wine tasting in the Valley. You can walk along the tasting rooms in downtown Solvang. You can take several wine trail maps and follow those, or pick up the Sideways map, produced by the Santa Barbara Conference and Visitors Bureau and Film Commission by calling (805) 966-9222.

During the movie, Jack and Miles visited **Foxen Winery, 7200 Foxen Canyon Road in nearby Santa Maria, (805) 937-4251.** Foxen is where Jack and Miles help themselves to a full glass of wine when the pourer has her back turned.

Firestone is where Miles, Jack, Stephanie and Maya sneak out of a wine tour and take a private tour of the barrel room.

Fess Parker's Winery and Vineyard was also featured in the movie disguised as Frass Canyon. The winery is best remembered as the place where a distraught Miles guzzles the contents of a spit bucket after the pourer refuses to pour him a full glass of wine.

Kalyra Winery is where Miles and Jack meet Stephanie and at **Sanford**, Miles teaches Jack the basics of wine tasting. If you go to Sanford you may even meet Chris Burroughs, he was the rugged wine pourer in the movie. He's often there wearing his cowboy hat, pouring wine and singing the praises of Pinot Noir.

From rustic barns to chateau-like facilities, Valley wineries come in all shapes, sizes and themes. Along with fine wines many have shops that sell collectibles, logo merchandise and edibles. Most of them don't sell food, and there really isn't any place to buy food along the wine trails.

If you're in for a day of wine tasting I'd recommend bringing a lunch. While there's no place to buy food, there are plenty of wineries that offer picnic areas.

Going in a group is fun but even if you're alone, you may be surprised at the end of the day to realize you've made a host of new friends. You'll tend to see the same faces as you travel from winery to winery.

Another tip: Toward the end of the day tasters get testy. There's often a mad rush to get to from tasting rooms that are closing to the ones that are open a half hour or so later. Closing time is also the most crowded time with people anxious to get a last taste of their favorite wines.

The Santa Barbara County Vintner's Association has maps available by calling (805) 688-0881 or visiting http://www.sbcountywines.com/visiting/map.htm.

Don't miss the opportunity to taste one of the many fine Pinot Noirs, for which the Valley has become known.

Directory of Wineries

Alexander and Wayne
2923 Grand Avenue, Los Olivos
11-6 daily
(805) 688-9665 (800) 824-8584
Picnic area
Chardonnay, Sauvignon Blanc, Pinot Noir, Merlot and
Cabernet.

Andrew Murray Vineyards
2901-A Grand Avenue, Los Olivos
11-6 daily, closed Tuesday.
Winery tours:11-4, Fri-Sun, (Apr-Oct)
(805) 686-9604
info@andrewmurrayvineyards.com
http://www.andrewmurrayvineyards.com/
Andrew Murray Vineyards is Santa Barbara County's only
exclusively Rhône varietal estate

Beckmen
2670 Ontiveros Road, Los Olivos
(805) 688-8664
beckmen@syv.com
http://www.beckmenvineyards.com/
Picnic area
Ultra-premium, estate grown Rhône varietal wines.

Bernat Vineyards & Winery
2879 Grand Avenue, Los Olivos
11-8 daily
805.688.7265, ex. 206
loscafe@silcom.com
http://www.santabarbarawine.com/

Blackjack Ranch Vineyards & Winery
2205 Alamo Pintado Road, Solvang
11-5 Fri-Sun. Summer, 11-5 daily.
(805) 686-9922 (866) 252-2522
bjranchrog@aol.com
http://www.blackjackranch.com/
Picnic area

The Brander Vineyard
Domaine Santa Barbara
Highway 154 at Roblar, Los Olivos
10-5 daily Summer, 10-4 daily Winter
(805) 688-2455 (800) 970-9979
info@brander.com
http://www.brander.com/
Picnic area
Bordeaux varietals, featuring world class Sauvignon Blancs.

Brophy Clark Cellars
2905 Grand Avenue, Los Olivos
11-6 daily
(805) 929-4830
info@brophyclark.com
http://www.brophyclarkcellars.com/
Pinot Noir, Syrah, Zinfandel and Sauvignon Blanc.

Byron Vineyard & Winery
Tastings at the winery by appointment only,
10am to 3pm Monday to Friday
call 1.888.303.7288 for advance reservations.
Tastings also available at the Santa Ynez Inn Wine Cellar,
3631 Sagunto Street, Santa Ynez
(805) 688-8688
info@byronwines.com
http://www.byronwines.com/
Chardonnay, Pinot Noir, Pinot Blanc and Pinot Gris.

Carhartt Vineyard
2905 Grand Avenue, Los Olivos
11-6 daily
(805) 688-0685
info@carharttvineyard.com
http://www.carharttvineyard.com/
Merlot and Syrah.

Carina Cellars
2900 Grand Avenue, Suite A, Los Olivos
11am to 5pm, Thursday through Monday
(805) 688-2459
info@carinacellars.com
http://www.carinacellars.com/
Syrahs and Viognier

Casa Cassara Winery & Vineyard
PO Box 2007
Buellton, CA 93427
(805) 688-8691
alicia@ccwinery.com
http://www.casacassarawinery.com/
Pinot Noir from the Santa Rita Hills appellation.

Clos Pepe Estate
Tasting at the Los Olivos Wine & Spirits Emporium
2531 Grand Ave, Los Olivos (888) 729-4637
11-6 daily
weshagen@thegrid.net
http://www.clospepe.com/
805-735-2196
Pinot Noir and Chablis-style Chardonnay (non-oaked)

Cold Heaven
PO Box 113
Los Olivos, CA 93441
(805) 937-9801
info@coldheavencellars.com
http://www.coldheavencellars.com
Tasting available at the Los Olivos Wine & Spirits Emporium,
2531 Grand Ave, Los Olivos, CA
(805) 688-4409

Consilience
2933 Grand Avenue, Los Olivos
11-5 daily
(805) 691-1020
info@consiliencewines.com
http://www.consiliencewines.com/

Curtis Winery
5249 Foxen Canyon Road, Los Olivos
10-5 daily.
(805) 686-8999
info@curtiswinery.com
http://www.curtiswinery.com/
Picnic area. 1.2 mile hiking trail connects Curtis to Firestone
Vineyard.
Rhône varietals.

Daniel Gehrs Wines
2939 Grand Avenue, Los Olivos
(at Heather Cottage)
11-6 daily
(805) 693-9686 (800) 275-8138
dgwines@syv.com
http://www.dgwines.com/
Syrah, Pinot Noir, Cabernet Sauvignon, Cabernet Franc,
Merlot, Chenin Blanc, Viognier, Pinot Blanc and Grenache.

Dierberg Vineyard
2905 Grand Avenue, Los Olivos
(805) 693-0744
wineinfo@dierbergvineyard.com
http://www.dierbergvineyard.com/
Pinot Noir and Chardonnay.

Epiphany Cellars
2963 Grand Avenue, Los Olivos
Thu - Mon, 11.30am - 5.30pm
(805) 686-2424 (866) 354-9463
kathy@epiphanycellars.com
http://www.epiphanycellars.com/

Fess Parker Winery & Vineyard
6200 Foxen Canyon Road, Los Olivos
10-5 daily. Tours: 11, 1, 3
(805) 688-1545 (800) 841-1104
fparker@fessparker.com
http://www.fessparker.com/
Picnic area
Syrah, Viognier, Pinot Noir, Chardonnay and White Riesling.

Fiddlehead Cellars
(530) 756-4550
headfiddle@fiddleheadcellars.com
http://www.fiddleheadcellars.com/
Tasting available at the Los Olivos Wine & Spirits Emporium,
2531 Grand Ave, Los Olivos, CA
(805) 688-4409
Pinot Noir, Sauvignon Blanc.

Firestone Vineyard
5000 Zaca Station Rd., Los Olivos
10-5 daily. Tours: 10:15 -3:15, quarter past each hour
(805) 688-3940
info@FirestoneWine.com
http://www.firestonewine.com/
Picnic area, hiking trail.

Flying Goat Cellars
2531 Grand Avenue, Los Olivos
11-6 daily
800-68WINES
ynot@flyinggoatcellars.com
http://www.flyinggoatcellars.com/
(805) 688.1814 Pinot Noir.

Foley Estates Vineyard & Winery
1711 Alamo Pintado Rd., Solvang
10-5 daily
(805) 688-8554
info@foleywines.com
http://www.foleywines.com/
Picnic area
Pinot Noir, Chardonnay, Sauvignon Blanc, Cabernet
Sauvignon and Merlot.

The Gainey Vineyard
3950 E. Hwy 246, Santa Ynez
10-5 daily Tours: 11, 1, 2, 3.
(805) 688-0558
info@gaineyvineyard.com
http://www.gaineyvineyard.com/
Picnic area
Chardonnay, Sauvignon Blanc, Riesling, Merlot, Cabernet
Franc and Pinot Noir.

Hitching Post Wines
406 E Hwy 246, Buellton
4-6 pm daily
(805) 688-0676
frank@hitchingpostwines.com
http://www.hitchingpostwines.com/
Pinot Noir, Syrah and Chardonnay.

Huber Vineyards
2531 Grand Avenue, Los Olivos
11-6 daily
(805) 736-3854
hubervineyards@yahoo.com
http://www.hubervineyards.com/

Io
Tastings at the winery by appointment only,
10am to 3pm Monday to Friday
call 1.888.303.7288 for advance reservations
Tasting available at the Santa Ynez Inn Wine Cellar, 3631
Sagunto Street, Santa Ynez
(805) 688-8688
info@iowine.com

J. Kerr Wines
2905 Grand Avenue, Los Olivos
11-6 daily
(805) 688-5337
jkwines@msn.com
Chardonnay and Syrah.

Koehler Winery
5360 Foxen Cyn Rd, Los Olivos
10-5 daily
(805) 693-8384
info@koehlerwinery.com
http://www.koehlerwinery.com/
Picnic area
Sauvignon Blanc, Chardonnay, Syrah, Cabernet Sauvignon, Riesling and Sangiovese.

Lafond Winery & Vineyards
6855 Santa Rosa Road, Buellton
10-5 daily
(805) 688-7921
1-877-708-9463
fax (805) 693-1524
lwv@lafondwinery.com
http://www.lafondwinery.com/
Picnic area
Pinot Noir, Syrah and Chardonnay.

Lincourt Vineyards
1711 Alamo Pintado Rd., Solvang
10-5 daily
(805) 688-8554
info@lincourtwines.com
http://www.lincourtwines.com/
Picnic area
Pinot Noir and Chardonnay.

Longoria Wines
2935 Grand Avenue, Los Olivos
11-4:30 Fri-Sun 12-4:30 Mon-Thu
Closed Tues.
(805) 688-0305 (866) RL WINES (759-4637)
info@longoriawine.com
http://www.longoriawine.com/
Picnic area
Chardonnay, Pinot Noir, Merlot, Syrah and Cabernet Franc.

Lucas & Lewellen Vineyards
1645 Copenhagen Drive, Solvang
11-6 Mon-Sat, 12-6 Sun
(805) 344-3000 (888) 777-6663
info@llwine.com
http://www.llwine.com/

Mandolina
1665 Copenhagen Drive, Solvang
(805) 686-5506
11am to 6pm daily
info@llwine.com
http://www.llwine.com/
Californian-Italian varieties.

Morovino
433 Alisal Road, Solvang
10-5 Thu-Mon
(805) 347-1272
http://www.morovino.com/
Zinfandel, Merlot, Barbera and Chardonnay.

Mosby Winery
9496 Santa Rosa Road, Buellton
10-4:30 daily
(805) 688-2415 (800) 706-6729
mosbywines@yahoo.com
http://www.mosbywines.com/
Picnic area
Sangiovese, Nebbiolo, Dolcetto, Pinot Grigio, Cortese,
Teroldego and award-winning Grappa.

Oak Savanna Wines
PO Box 687
Los Olivos, CA 93441
office@oaksavannawine.com
http://www.oaksavannawine.com/
Chardonnay and Syrah, Pinot Noir and Cabernet Sauvignon.

Paige 23 Wines
PO Box 1313
Solvang, CA 93464
(805) 686-0015
http://www.paige23wines.com/

Qupé
PO Box 440
Los Olivos, CA 93441
(805) 937-9801
bob@qupe.com
http://www.qupe.com/
Tasting available at Los Olivos Wine & Spirits Emporium,
2531 Grand Ave, Los Olivos, CA
(805) 688-4409
Syrah, Viognier, Marsanne, Roussanne, Chardonnay.

Rideau Vineyard
1562 Alamo Pintado Road, Solvang
11-5 pm daily
(805) 688-0717
rideauvineyard@aol.com
http://www.rideauvineyard.com/
Picnic area

Royal Oaks Winery
1651 Copenhagen Drive, Solvang, CA
(805) 693-1740
10am to 5.30pm daily
info@royaloakswinery.com
http://www.royaloakswinery.com/

Rusack Vineyards
1819 Ballard Canyon Road, Solvang
11-5 daily. Winter hours may vary.
(805) 688-1278
wine@rusackvineyards.com
http://www.rusackvineyards.com/
Picnic area

Sanford Winery & Vineyards
7250 Santa Rosa Road, Buellton
11-4 daily
Picnic area
(805) 688-3300 (800) 426-9463
sanford@silcom.com
http://www.sanfordwinery.com/
Pinot Noir and Chardonnay.

Star Lane
 (805) 693-0744
wineinfo@starlanevineyard.com
http://www.starlanevineyard.com/
Cabernet Sauvignon, Cabernet Franc, Merlot, Malbec and
Petit Verdot.

Stolpman
1659 Copenhagen Drive, Suite C, Solvang
(805) 688-0400
from 11am daily
info@stolpmanvineyards.com
http://www.stolpmanvineyards.com/

Sunstone Vineyards & Winery
125 Refugio Road, Santa Ynez
10-4 daily
(805) 688-9463 (800) 313-9463
http://www.sunstonewinery.com/
Sauvignon Blanc, Chardonnay, Viognier, Merlot, Syrah,
Cabernet Franc and uniquely blended reds.

Tantara Winery
2531 Grand Avenue Los Olivos
11-6 daily
(805) 938-5050
tantara@tantarawinery.com
http://www.tantarawinery.com/
Pinot Noir and Chardonnay.

Vandale Vineyards
2531 Grand Avenue, Los Olivos
11-6 daily
(805) 688-0255
vanwine@silcom.com
Sangiovese.

Verdad Wine Cellars
PO Box 440
Los Olivos, CA 934441
(805) 937-9801
louisa@qupe.com
http://www.verdadwines.com/
Tasting available at Los Olivos Wine & Spirits Emporium,
2531 Grand Ave, Los Olivos, CA
(805) 688-4409
Tempranillo and Albariño.

Whitcraft Winery
Tasting Room: 2531 Grand Avenue Los Olivos
11-6 daily
(805) 688-4409
Tastings also at 819 East Montecito Street, Santa Barbara
Friday - Sunday, 12-4
whitcraftwinery@cox.net
http://www.whitcraftwinery.com/
(805) 965-0956

Zaca Mesa Winery
6905 Foxen Canyon Road, Los Olivos
10-4 daily
(805) 688-9339 (800) 350-7972
zmail@zacamesa.com
http://www.zacamesa.com/
Picnic area. Private tours by appointment.
Syrah, Grenache, Viognier and Mourvedre, along with our
delicious Chardonnay.

Events You Can't Miss

Solvang Century Bike Ride

During March Solvang hosts the Solvang Century Bike Ride. Thousands of cyclists from all over the country begin and end their 100-mile ride in Solvang. The city comes alive with the revelry and excitement of these adventurers.

Taste of Solvang

Want a great way to get a quick introduction to Solvang? Join the "Taste of Solvang" the weekend food festival includes a Dessert Reception, Walking Smorgasbord and Wine and Cheese Tasting with live entertainment throughout the Village. Tickets are required and allow the holder to visit several merchants to taste their wares. The event sells out fast.

For more information call, the Solvang Conference and Visitors Bureau, 800-468-6765.

Vintner's Festival

In April, vintners celebrate spring with the Vintner's Festival held each year at the Firestone Crossroads Meadows. More than 70 wineries and restaurants set up at the Firestone Meadow for a day of tasting local wines, sampling food and enjoying the best entertainment the Valley has to offer. Tickets are sold in advance only and sell out quick.

Call (805) 688-0881 or (800) 218-0881.

Los Rancheros Visitadores

In May, Los Rancheros Visitadores, said to be the largest riding group of its kind in the world with hundreds of riders participating, makes its annual ride to the Old Mission Santa Ines for the blessing of their horses by padres. 800-468-6765.

PCPA Theaterfest

From June to October the PCPA Theaterfest Season takes place presenting critically acclaimed live theater. Solvang boasts an outdoor amphitheater so patrons view performances under the stars.

For ticket information, call (805) 922-8313.

Old Santa Ynez Day

In June, Old Santa Ynez Day makes the Old West come alive with a parade, food and entertainment. Call (805) 688-878.

Old Mission Santa Ines Fiesta

If you're in Solvang in August don't miss out on the Old Mission Santa Ines Fiesta. The event offers food and festivities, folklorico dancers, mariachis and a wide array of local entertainment. Call (805) 688-4815.

Danish Days

In September Solvang shines as it shares its Danish heritage with visitors in a unique way. Danish Days is a weekend showcasing Danish food and costumes. Come grab an aebleskiver and join in a folk dance. The event includes a parade, food and dancing. Definitely a must to experience. (805) 688-6144 or 800-468-6765.

Celebration of Harvest

In October the Valley celebrates harvest with the Celebration of Harvest. A day of wine and gourmet food among nature's beauty. (805) 688-0881 or 800-218-0881.

Los Olivos Day in the Country

Later in the month of October Los Olivos celebrates its art community with an old-fashioned celebration during Los Olivos Day in the Country. Come experience the art, crafts, food and fun. (805) 688-1222.

Vaquero Show and Sale

In November, Santa Ynez hosts the Vaquero Show and Sale. Find western and cowboy antiques and collectibles featuring noted artisans and cowboy art. (805) 688-7889.

Winterfest

Christmastime is magical in Solvang. Don't miss the Winterfest Celebration, which begins in mid-November and continues until Christmas. Special events are planned all season and Santa Claus makes regular appearances throughout the Village. Call (805) 688-6144 or 800-468-6765 for a Winterfest schedule of events.

Resources

City of Solvang
http://www.cityofsolvang.com/
(805) 688-5575

Solvang Chamber of Commerce
http://www.solvangcc.com/
(805) 688-0701

Solvang Conference and Visitors Bureau
http://www.solvangusa.com/
800-468-6765

Buellton Chamber of Commerce
http://www.buellton.org/
800-324-3800

City of Buellton
http://www.cityofbuellton.com/
(805) 686-0137

Santa Barbara County Vintner's Association
http://www.sbcountywines.com/
(805) 688-0881

About the Author

Shelly Cone has spent most of her years exploring California's coastal beauty and scenic valleys. A frequent traveler, the Santa Ynez Valley remains her favorite place to play. In her previous life, Shelly was a newspaper reporter and editor having written on everything from politics to lifestyle features. She now divides her time between her family and finding an ever-better pinot noir.

Readers are invited to share their wine country stories or experiences, reviews of hotels, wineries or restaurants (both enjoyable and not so enjoyable) or comments, to Shelly at sugarcone2@verizon.net. Your comments may be helpful for future editions.

Printed in the United Kingdom
by Lightning Source UK Ltd.
115339UKS00001B/8